The Ultimate Drum Machine Coloring B

By Adam J Garner and DJ LimeGreen

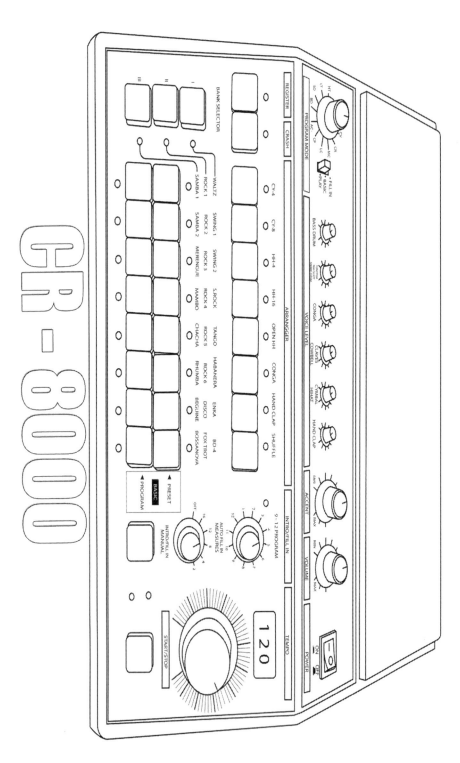

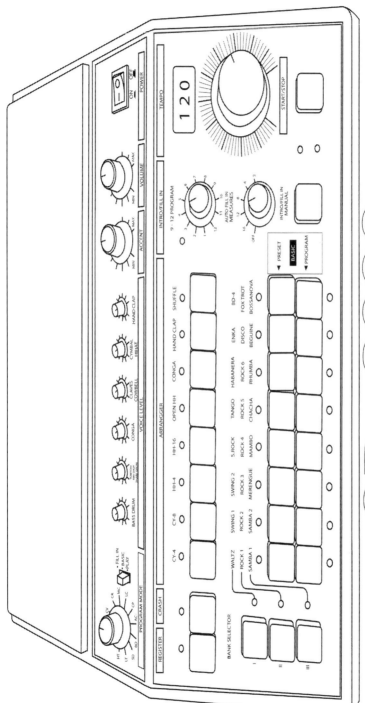

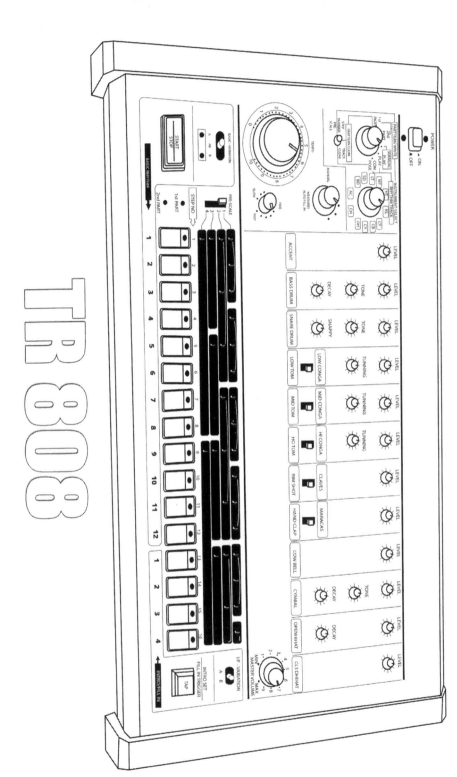

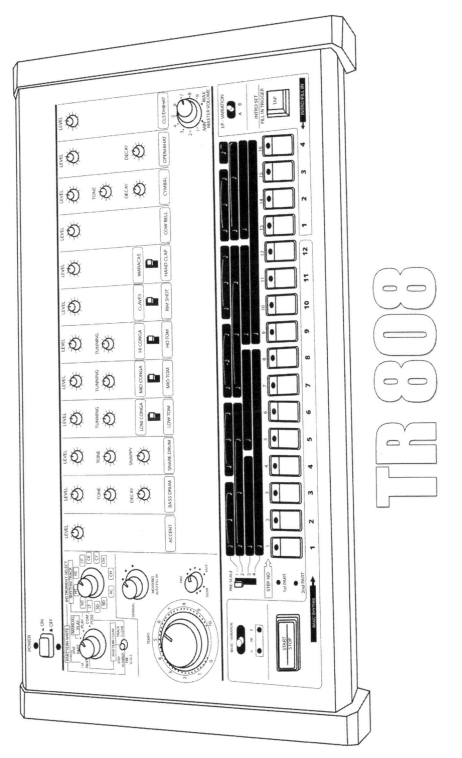

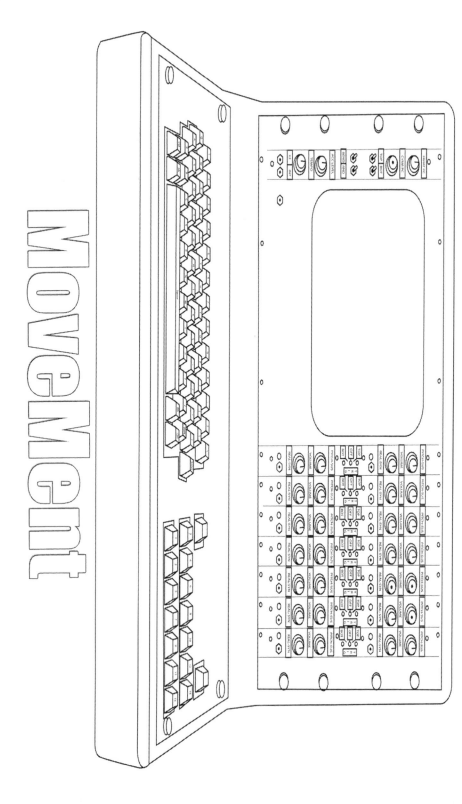

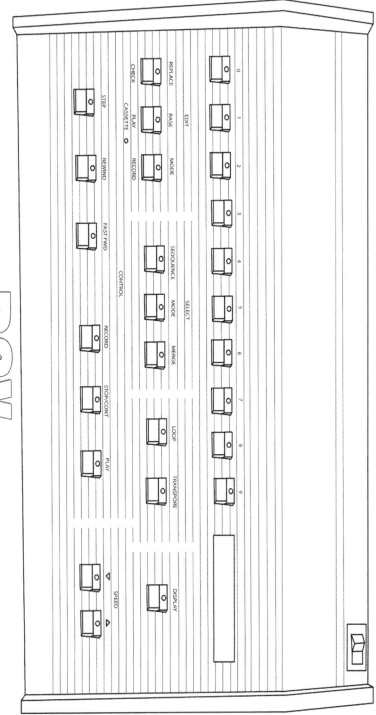

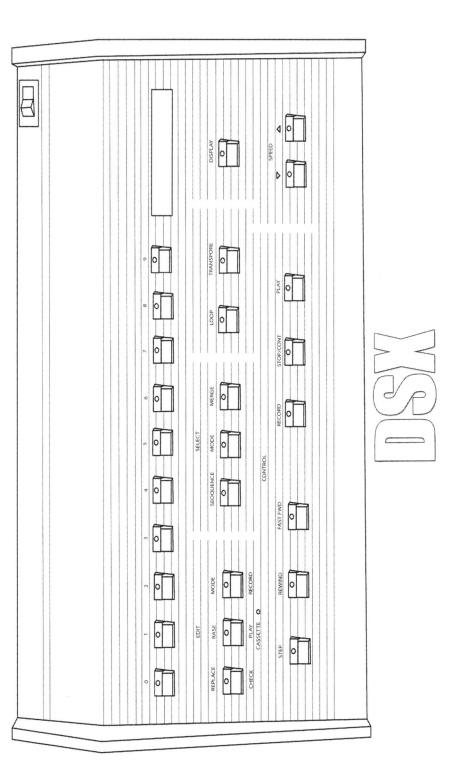

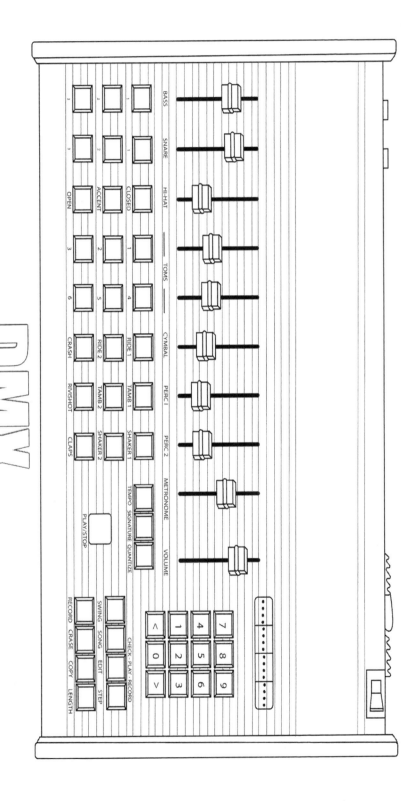

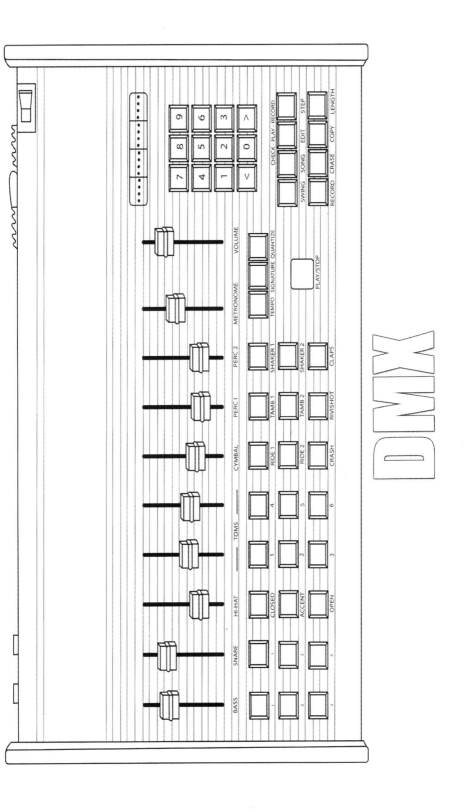

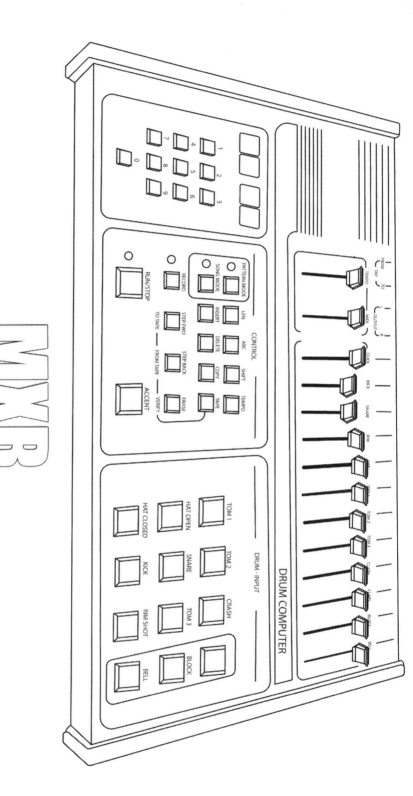

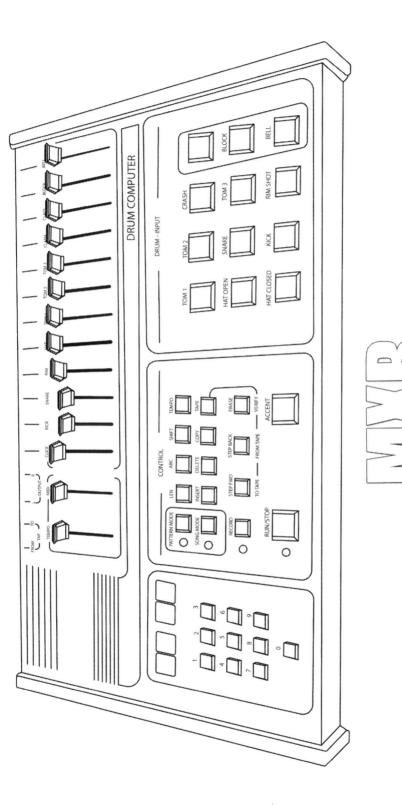

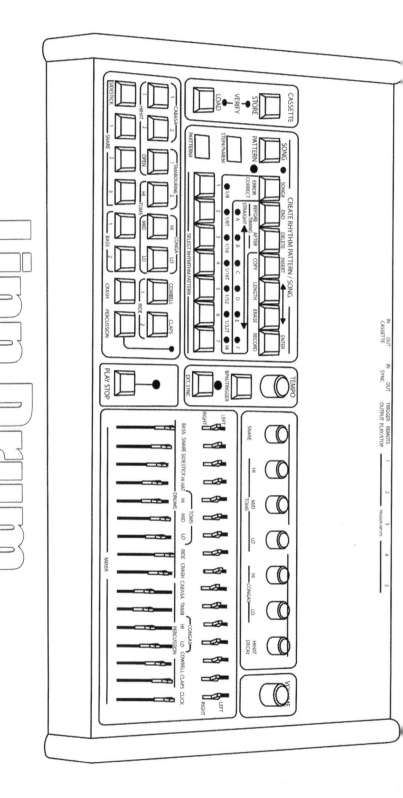

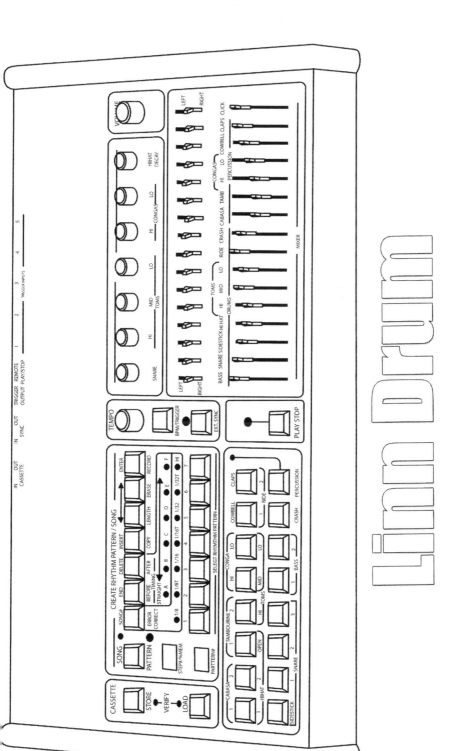

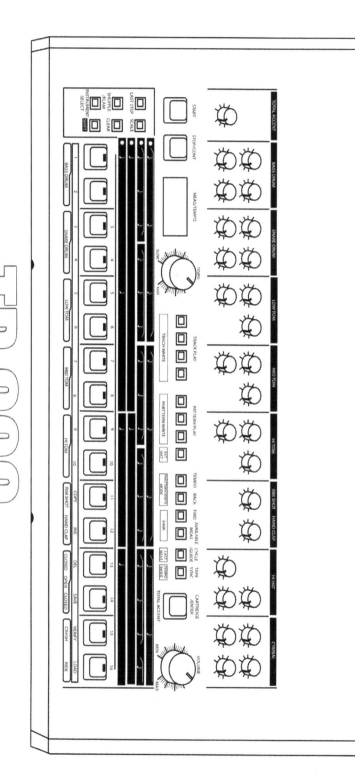

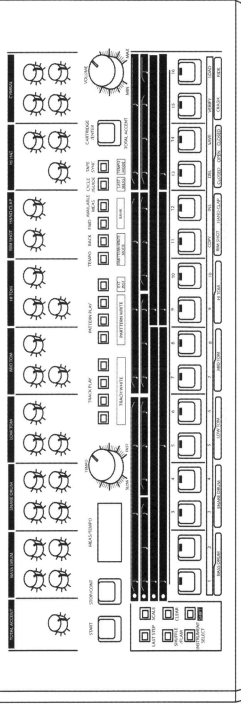

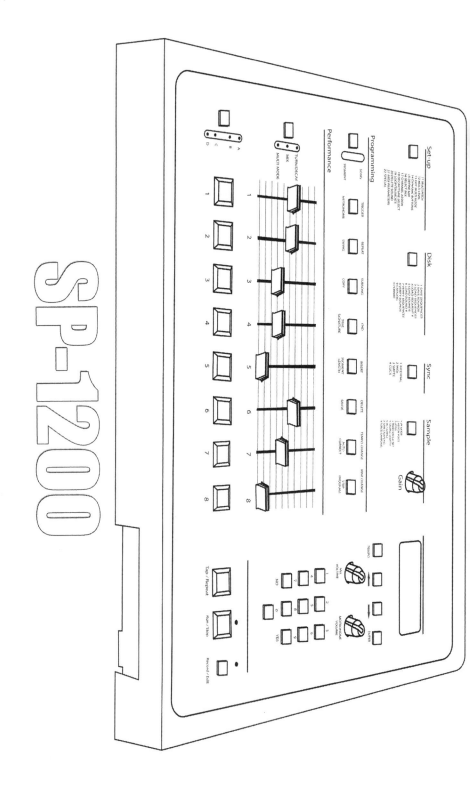

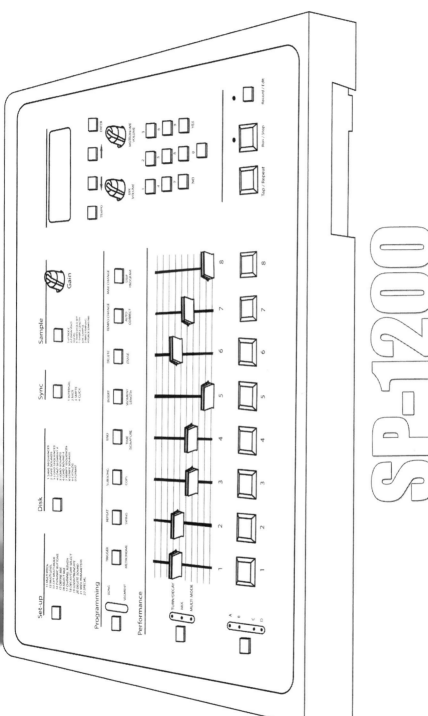

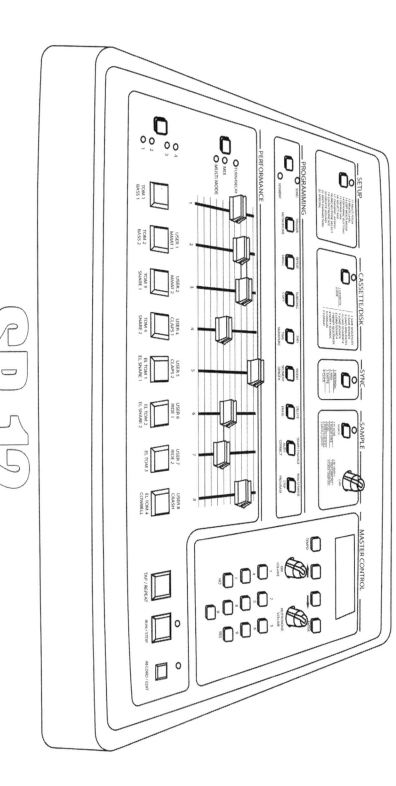

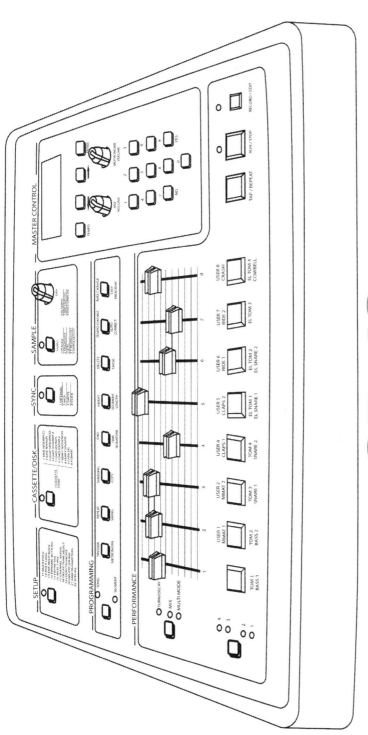

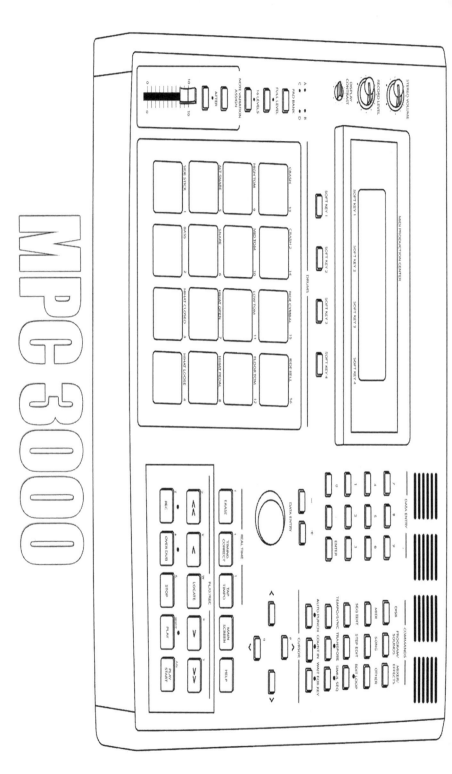

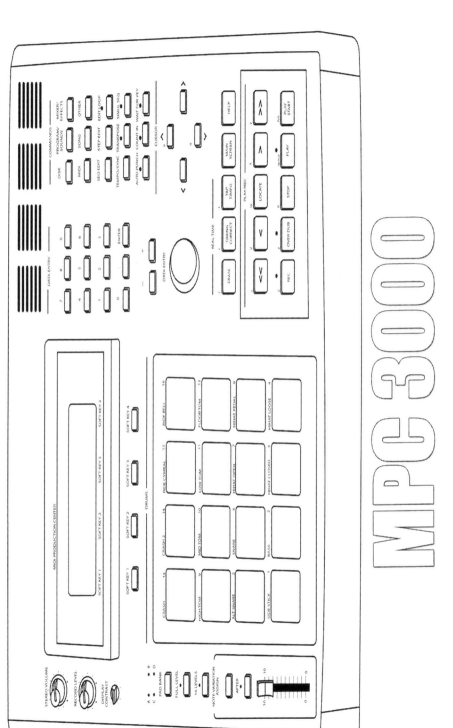

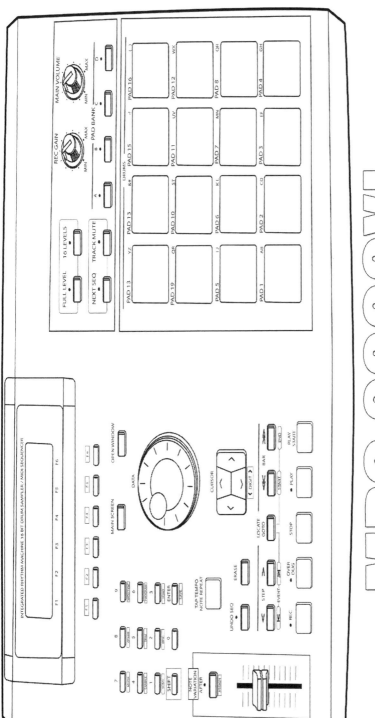

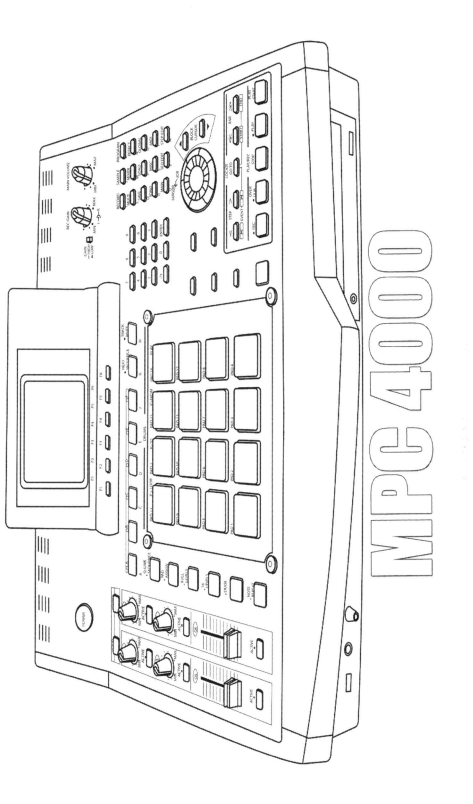

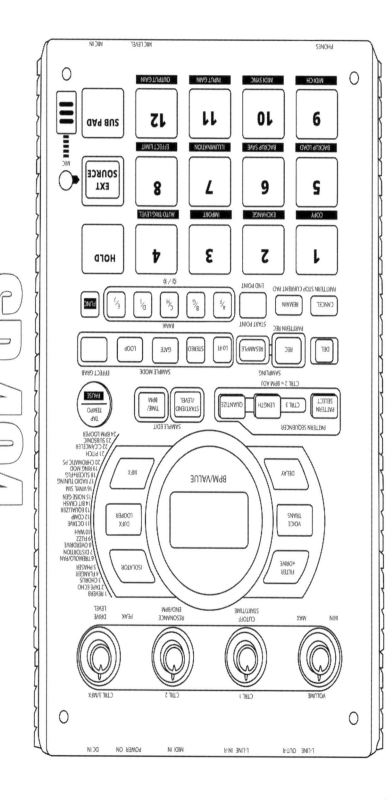

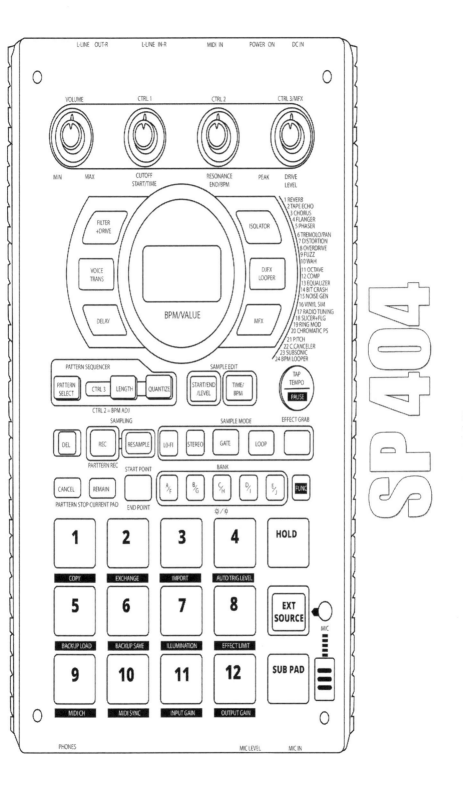

TUNEK

TUNEK

TUNEK

TUNEK

TUNEK

DUEM

"style" by Izze WST

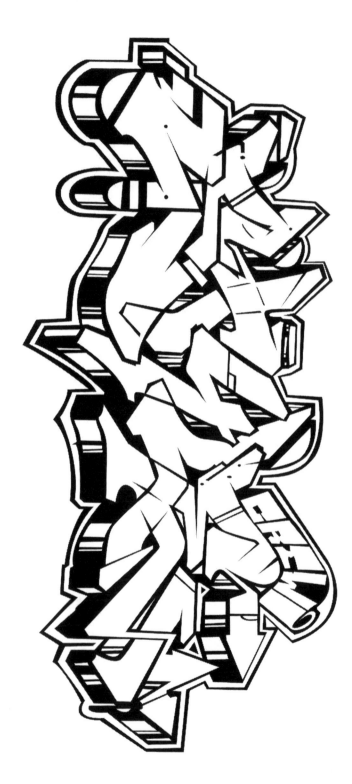

"Style" by Izze WST

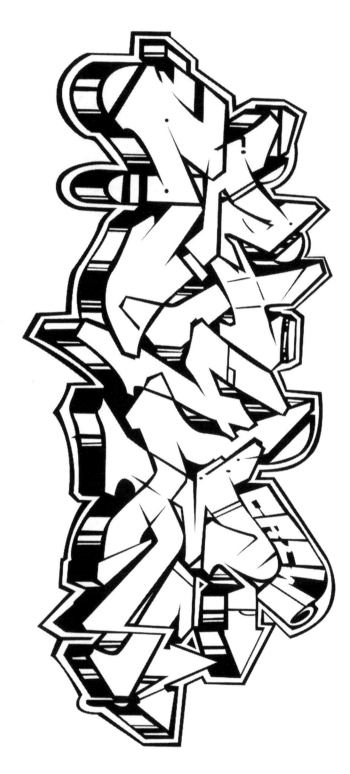

"style" by Izze WST

"Style" by Izze WST

"The Green Room" Damet Tewsr*Note

"The Green Room" Damet Tewsr Note

Made in the USA
Columbia, SC
15 July 2023

20069649R00028